FR. JACQUES PHILIPPE

LESSONS *for* SHARING THE GOSPEL

Copyright © 2026 Jacques Philippe

All rights reserved.

Published by The Word Among Us Press

7115 Guilford Drive, Suite 100

Frederick, Maryland 21704

wau.org

30 29 28 27 26   1 2 3 4 5

ISBN: 978-1-59325-745-3

eISBN: 978-1-59325-746-0

Unless otherwise noted, Scripture texts in this work are taken from The Catholic Edition of the Revised Standard Version of the Bible, copyright © 1965, 1966 National Council of the Churches of Christ in the United States of America. Used by permission. All rights reserved worldwide.

Scripture texts marked NABRE are taken from the New American Bible, revised edition © 2010, 1991, 1986, 1970 Confraternity of Christian Doctrine, Washington, D.C., and are used by permission of the copyright owner. All rights reserved. No part of the New American Bible may be reproduced in any form without permission in writing from the copyright owner.

Design by Rose Audette

No part of this publication may be reproduced, stored in a retrieval system, or transmitted in any form or by any means—electronic, mechanical, photocopy, recording, or any other—except for brief quotations in printed reviews, without the prior permission of the author and publisher.

Library of Congress Control Number: 2026900844

Contents

1. Bearers of God's Love and Compassion 5
2. The Power of Prayer 9
3. The Importance of Charity 13
4. A Mission to Love One Another 15
5. With the Holy Spirit 19
6. Practical Ways to Evangelize 23
7. Bearing Witness in Suffering 27
8. Sharing the Fragrance of Christ 33
9. Entrusting Ourselves to Mary 39
10. Q & A with Fr. Jacques Philippe 45
11. Books by Fr. Jacques Philippe 51

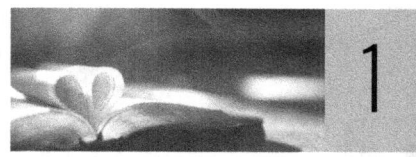

Bearers of God's Love and Compassion

In Matthew 9:36, we see that Jesus was moved with compassion when he saw the crowds that were "harassed and helpless, like sheep without a shepherd." As his disciples, he wants us to share his heart for people—to be witnesses to his compassion.

Every sincere Christian must ask themselves, "How can I, today, be a witness to the gospel?" As we consider how to evangelize, we can see that there are many different ways to share the good news. But first and foremost, we need to know that evangelization must proceed not just from good ideas or convictions that we want everyone to share. It must come from a deep compassion for the suffering in the world, as well as a personal experience of God's love and a living relationship with Jesus. Indeed the first duty of the one who wants to evangelize is not to develop techniques but to seek union with God and intimacy with Christ in prayer, so that God can make each person feel the deep compassion he has for them.

The first duty of the one who wants to evangelize is not to develop techniques but to seek union with God and intimacy with Christ in prayer.

When we share the gospel with others, we should feel what Paul felt when he told the Corinthians:

> For though I am free from all men, I made myself a slave to all, that I might win the more. To the Jews I became as a Jew, in order to win Jews; to those under the law I became as one under the law—though not being under the law—that I might win those under the law. To those outside the law I became as one outside the law—not being without law toward God but under the law of Christ—that I might win those outside the law. To the weak I became weak, that I might win the weak. I have become all things to all men, that I might by all means save some. I do it all for the sake of the gospel, that I may share in its blessings. (1 Corinthians 9:19-23)

Reflect

How have you experienced God's love and compassion in your life? How has it helped you?

What do you think St. Paul meant when he wrote that he had become "a slave to all" and "all things to all men" in order to win people to Christ? How does this challenge you as you consider how to present the gospel to the people in your life?

Pray About

What are one or two small steps you can take to be a witness to God's love and compassion to those around you?

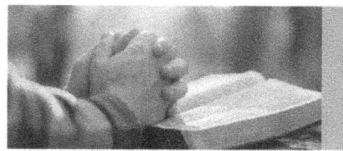

The Power of Prayer

Prayer is a fundamental requirement for true evangelization. It puts us in contact with God and makes us share in the love he has for mankind. As St. John of the Cross put it, the deeper our prayer life, the more we will feel compassion for people:

> The more compassion one has for one's neighbor, the more the soul unites itself to God, through love; for the more it loves, the more it desires that this same God be loved and honored by all. And the more it desires it, the more it works for it, both in prayer and by all the other necessary means which are possible. And in those who are thus possessed by God, the fervor and strength for their charity are such that they cannot be satisfied with their own benefit. But however as it seems little for them to go to heaven alone, they seek with anguish, with a love that is all heavenly, and with an exquisite eagerness to take to heaven with them a great number of souls. All this is born of the great love they have for their God. It is the proper fruit and effect of perfect prayer and contemplation.[1]

---

1 St. John of the Cross, *Oeuvres Completes [Complete Works]* (Paris, France: Desclée de Brouwer, 1959), 1027, passage translated by the author.

It is the duty of everyone who wants to evangelize to let himself be filled with the love of God, especially through intimacy with God through prayer. We have the example of St. Thérèse of Lisieux, who became patroness of the missions without ever having left her Carmel. Thérèse was a great evangelizer through her sacrifices and prayers. She was convinced of the fruitfulness of prayer. "The power of prayer is certainly wonderful," she said. "One might liken it to a queen who always has free access to the king and can obtain everything she asks."[2]

This reality of the power of prayer is very consoling and comforting because we cannot always talk to people or convince them, but we can always pray for them. When our human means are lacking, we always have prayer to enable us to reach people in their difficulties and needs. This way of leading souls to God will always be available to us! Even when we are sick or old, we will always have this opportunity to visit everyone on earth through our prayers. This is so comforting and encouraging!

Prayer is also an authentic form of spiritual motherhood or fatherhood. As a mother watches over her sick child, we are called to carry our poor world in our hearts and in our prayers. We can recall the beautiful words of the prophet Isaiah. God says through the prophet,

---

[2] Thomas J. Craughwell, *30 Days with Saint Thérèse* (Charlotte, NC: TAN Books, 2012), page 20.

> Upon your walls, O Jerusalem,
>   I have set watchmen,
> all the day and all the night
>   they shall never be silent.
> You who put the Lord in remembrance,
>   take no rest,
> and give him no rest,
>   until he establishes Jerusalem
> and makes it a praise in the earth. (62:6-7)

These words invite us to pray and to intercede without ceasing, to give God no rest "until he establishes Jerusalem and makes it a praise in the earth." This is also our duty. By our Baptism, we have a priesthood and a call to intercession—not to give God rest until he fulfills his promise of mercy for the world.

Reflect

St. John of the Cross wrote about how our love for God, born of prayer and contemplation, should lead us to be eager "to take to heaven with [us] a great number of souls." Have you found this to be true in your own life? Has a deeper prayer life led you to grow in love for others, particularly for them to know the love of God and the joy of being bound for heaven?

"We cannot always talk to people or convince them, but we can always pray for them." Have you considered that this way of leading souls to God is always available to you?

Pray About

How might you deepen your prayer life and draw even closer to God?

Who is the Holy Spirit guiding you to pray for today? What is your hope for this person?

The Importance of Charity

The proclamation of the gospel must always be accompanied by a gentle and tender charity toward people. We must not forget that the most convincing witness will always be the witness of charity. The language of love is the most universal language. Everyone understands the language of love. Evangelization must always be accompanied by concern for the poor, the little ones, the suffering, and the most vulnerable.

Reflect

> Have you found it challenging to keep a "gentle and tender charity" in your efforts to share your faith? How can a concern for the most vulnerable increase your ability to share your faith with love?

Pray About

> How might you help someone in need?

A Mission to Love One Another

Evangelization must always be done in communion with the Church. It is not a personal initiative, but a mission received from the Church and lived in communion with the leaders of the Church. Knowing that we are sent by the Church and therefore by Christ himself gives us a special strength.

In addition, it is important that we not be alone, but that we rely on our brothers and sisters. Jesus sent the disciples on mission two by two. The witness of brotherly love is a great strength for the proclamation of the gospel. "Love one another," Jesus said. "By this all men will know that you are my disciples" (John 13:34-35). This means that when there is division, jealousy, comparison, judgment, or competition, it will be difficult to proclaim the gospel. So we have to be very attentive to this—that we love one another and that we not have any jealousy, comparison, or judgment toward anyone.

We have to be very attentive to this—that we love one another and that we not have any jealousy, comparison, or judgment toward anyone.

Reflect

When working or living closely with others, different personalities and priorities can make it hard to love one another. How can Jesus' words—"By this all men will know that you are my disciples"—increase your desire to overcome temptations toward jealousy, comparison, or judgment?

Pray About

Who are you being asked to forgive and ask forgiveness from?

With the Holy Spirit

We must also remember the importance of the role of the Holy Spirit in evangelizing. Evangelization can only be done with the grace of the Holy Spirit. It is a work that is absolutely beyond human abilities. It has nothing to do with communication techniques, and it is not about attracting people or convincing them with well-prepared arguments. It is about leading people to a living experience of God's presence and a love that transforms the heart. Only the Holy Spirit can do this! Only he can give people a living experience of God's presence and love. We see how, after Pentecost, Peter addressed the crowd, and those who listened to him were "cut to the heart" because the words Peter spoke came directly from the Holy Spirit (Acts 2:37). Only the Holy Spirit is powerful enough to do that!

This means that the first duty of the person who is called to evangelize is not to develop efficient techniques, but to be converted. He or she must strive to acquire an inner attitude that makes them open and docile to the Holy Spirit. It is very

Evangelization is about leading people to a living experience of God's presence and a love that transforms the heart. Only the Holy Spirit can do this!

important that we understand and practice the inner attitudes that make us open to the grace of the Holy Spirit.

This openness to the Holy Spirit includes faithfulness to prayer, faith and trust without limits, poverty of heart, purity of intention, and humility. God "opposes the proud, but gives grace to the humble," St. James writes (4:6). So for those who want to proclaim the gospel, the urgency is not to acquire the right technique, but that their hearts be purified and rid of all pride, human ambition, and self-seeking. As the heart becomes radically poor and free, it then has no other desire than serving God and no other support or security than God's grace. And what makes evangelization effective is not the richness of the means used, but poverty of heart, humility, charity, and trust in God alone.

Reflect

It is both a relief and a challenge to know that evangelization can only be done with the grace of the Holy Spirit. It's a relief that the conversion of people's hearts doesn't depend on our abilities, techniques, or efforts. At the same time, we are challenged to "acquire an inner attitude" that makes us "open and docile to the Holy Spirit," so that we can share our faith as the Holy Spirit prompts us.

Have you ever felt inadequate or burdened by the word "evangelization," seeing it as a weight you had to bear? Invite the Lord to reassure you that the work doesn't depend on your efforts and abilities.

Pray About

Are there any ways you may have pride, personal ambition, or selfish motives in your heart, particularly in the area of sharing your faith? If you do, renounce them, and surrender to the Holy Spirit, inviting him to mold your heart with greater trust, humility, and love—for yourself and for others.

Practical Ways to Evangelize

Practically speaking, there are many different ways to evangelize, and I think everyone has to discover their own path, asking the Holy Spirit to guide them. Each person can ask, *How, Lord, today—in my situation, in my life—can I be a part of the spreading of the gospel?* There are many different answers. Some people we will feel called to directly announce the gospel in different ways and to participate in evangelization activities such as teaching, catechesis, and faith formation. It has been very beautiful to see, for instance, how many people have taken the initiative to evangelize through the internet, especially since the Covid pandemic. Many laypeople have been very generous and creative in spreading the gospel in this way in the last few years.

God invites all of us to have a little more courage and boldness to witness to our faith, and to give the reason for the faith that lives in us. We can do this within our families, in our workplaces, and throughout our daily lives. God asks us, as it says in the First Letter of St. Peter, to "always be prepared to make a defense to

Everyone has to discover their own path for evangelizing, asking the Holy Spirit to guide them. Each person can ask, *How, Lord, today— in my situation, in my life—can I be a part of the spreading of the gospel?*

anyone who calls you to account for the hope that is in you" (3:15). St. Peter tells us that we must do it "with gentleness and reverence." In the times we are living in, people are more open to receiving this testimony of the hope and the love we have for Christ, and of the freedom and trust that we can find in the presence of Jesus in our lives.

Reflect

In what ways have you felt led to share your faith? Has it been through your parish or through your social media? Or perhaps with your family members or colleagues? Or even in your daily errands? Ask the Lord to give you creative ideas for how you can share the gospel even more effectively.

Pray About

Invite the Lord also to give you even more courage and boldness to witness to your faith, always with "gentleness and reverence."

Bearing Witness in Suffering

Another very powerful way to evangelize is through the offering of our suffering. Some people are called to this, and I believe that this is ultimately the most powerful of the means available to us. There are sometimes insurmountable walls of pride or hardness of heart that can only be pierced through the loving acceptance of the cross. Through the acceptance of our suffering, of our cross, we have the opportunity to announce Christ in hidden but real ways.

We will always have a suffering to offer, a struggle to accept, or a cross to say yes to. Always! We will then be able to take up the words of St. Paul to the Colossians: "Now I rejoice in my sufferings for your sake, and in my flesh I complete what is lacking in Christ's afflictions for the sake of his body, that is, the church" (Colossians 1:24).

Cardinal František Tomášek, the archbishop of Prague during the Communist regime, once said, "He who acts for the kingdom does much. He would prays for the kingdom does more. He who suffers for the kingdom does everything."

Through the acceptance of our suffering, of our cross, we have the opportunity to announce Christ in hidden but real ways.

We must recognize that evangelization also involves engaging in a spiritual battle. Inevitably, whoever wants to evangelize will experience difficulties, obstacles, temptations toward discouragement, insults, and other challenges. Paul makes this very clear in his letters when he tells the Colossians, "For I want you to know how greatly I strive for you, and for those at Laodicea, and for all who have not seen my face" (2:1). And he says to his disciple and coworker Timothy, "Take your share of suffering for the gospel in the power of God" (2 Timothy 1:8).

Sometimes, this suffering can go as far as martyrdom. Those who evangelize are witnesses—not to their own perfection, not to their own qualities. If that were the case, no one would be able to evangelize! We are witnesses to the mercy of God and the power of his love. And this witnessing sometimes finds expression in martyrdom. The acceptance of martyrdom is the strongest way to preach the gospel.

In the times to come, on the one hand it will be easier to evangelize because people's hearts will be more open. They will feel the need to draw closer to God in these difficult times. On the other hand, it will be also more challenging because of the hostility of the world toward the Church. We will see an increase in the contradiction between the message of the gospel and the mindset of our world, the Western world, which calls evil good and good evil. And it's possible that in some countries, including Western countries, Christians will be mistreated and persecuted.

We need to be ready for persecution. It will be the time to bear witness, not by our strength or moral superiority, but by the grace of the Holy Spirit, who comes to help us in our weakness.

It will be the time to bear witness, not by our strength or moral superiority, but by the grace of the Holy Spirit, who comes to help us in our weakness.

It will be the time to bear witness to our trust in God and to our attachment to Christ, with our eyes fixed on him. It will be the time to find in ourselves the capacity to bless those who curse us and to give our lives for our persecutors, as St. Stephen did. The story of his martyrdom is very beautiful. He "gazed into heaven and saw the glory of God, and Jesus standing at the right hand of God" (Acts 7:55). He fixed his eyes on Jesus, on Christ, and so he found the strength to forgive and to surrender himself like a child into the hands of Jesus. He fell asleep in death—in complete peace, in complete surrender to God, full of God's love and mercy for everyone.

Those who will be able to give this testimony will not be the wise and powerful according to the spirit of the world, but they will be the poor and little ones who have nothing to lose and nothing to fear because they belong to God. They also belong to the Blessed Virgin Mary, who will be their refuge and protection.

Reflect

Have you experienced persecution for your Christian faith? If so, how did you experience the grace of the Holy Spirit to help you bear witness to Christ and forgive those who came against you? If not, what can you learn from the example of St. Stephen in living fully surrendered to God?

Pray About

What suffering or struggle or cross can you accept and offer to the Lord? Take a moment to do that now.

Sharing the Fragrance of Christ

St. Paul writes in his Second Letter to the Corinthians:

> Thanks be to God, who in Christ always leads us in triumph, and through us spreads the fragrance of the knowledge of him everywhere. For we are the aroma of Christ. (2:14-15)

I really like this image—the Christian has to be a fragrance, a perfume of Christ. There is a way to lead people to Jesus, not by actions or by words, but simply by spreading the fragrance of the gospel—the good "smell" of Christ.

At our Baptism, we received the anointing of holy chrism, that oil consecrated by the bishop on Holy Thursday. In Eastern churches, Baptism of a child is done by immersion. After immersion of the child in water, the priest covers him or her from head to toe with holy chrism, and the smell spreads through the whole church. This is a beautiful symbol of Christian life. We must allow ourselves to be enveloped in the good odor of Christ, asking the Holy Spirit to perfume us with his anointing. What are the ingredients of this fragrance? Joy, simplicity,

There is a way to lead people to Jesus, not by actions or by words, but simply by spreading around us the fragrance of the gospel—the good "smell" of Christ.

humility, gentleness, purity, trust, mercy, peace, and hope. These are the main ingredients of the perfume of the gospel. This fragrance is a lifestyle, a way of being for those who belong to Christ and are anointed by the Holy Spirit.

We can find another beautiful description of this fragrance of Christ in the Gospel of Matthew, when Jesus says, "Blessed are the poor in spirit, . . . the meek, . . . the merciful, . . . the pure in heart" (5:3, 5, 7, 8). This is another way to describe the perfume of the gospel. We have to ask God to give us this anointing of the Beatitudes: the perfume of Christ.

What matters most is not what we do, but who we are. This is important—not what we say, not what we do, but who we are. And when we are so united to Christ through prayer, by love and by contemplation—when we are so anointed by the Holy Spirit to be capable to spread the fragrance of the gospel, then we can evangelize. We can even evangelize in silence! Even if one day we are forbidden from speaking, we will be able to continue evangelizing and spreading the perfume of Christ, the anointing of the Holy Spirit.

This fragrance of Christ is also prefigured in the Old Testament. In Psalm 45, the psalmist speaks about the messiah king:

> You love righteousness and hate wickedness.
> Therefore, God, your God, has anointed you
>   with the oil of gladness above your fellows;
> your robes are all fragrant with myrr and
>   aloes and cassia. (7-8)

This line is interesting: "You love righteousness and hate wickedness" (Psalm 45:7). This indicates that you have made a

May our lives be lived out of love, with perfume that spreads throughout the world and attracts hearts to Jesus.

choice—a whole-hearted choice—for God. And so the perfume can come out of your decision: for Christ and against evil and the spirit of the world. The way to receive this anointing is to make the choice for God, to make a whole-hearted decision for the gospel. In the times that are coming, we will be obliged to have a very strong commitment to the Lord, with no compromise or division in our hearts.

This perfume is also mentioned in the Song of Songs, which speaks of the beloved's name as "a flowing perfume" (1:3, NABRE). Let us also remember the beautiful scene of anointing in Bethany, a few days before Jesus' passion. As Mary breaks a bottle of precious perfume, out of her love for Jesus, "the house was filled with the fragrance of the oil" (John 12:3, NABRE). It's interesting, too, that Jesus himself makes the link between the spreading of this perfume and the proclamation of the gospel: "Amen, I say to you, wherever this gospel is proclaimed in the whole world, what she has done will be spoken of, in memory of her" (Matthew 26:13, NABRE). This is a beautiful image of the diffusion of the gospel.

Everyone will remember what this woman has done, her beautiful expression of her love. She was suffering, seeing the increasing hostility against Jesus. She felt that Jesus was about to be killed, to suffer, and she asked herself, "What can I do, as a woman? I cannot convince Pilate, I cannot speak to the high priest, but I will do what I can do—give my love, spread my love. I will give the most precious thing I have." She was completely powerless, but she had the power to give Jesus the deepest love, to console him and accompany him during his passion. This gesture was totally inefficient, but totally powerful, because it was love.

As St. John of the Cross said, a single act of pure love is more powerful than any action. We have to look for purity of love. And we will be true evangelizers if our hearts are pure.

So may our lives be lived out of love, with perfume that spreads throughout the world and attracts hearts to Jesus. In this way, we will be evangelizers even without opening our mouths. Even if we must be silent, we will still be evangelizing about Jesus.

Reflect

> If you ever attended a Baptism, you might remember the smell of the chrism that is placed on the baby or believer's head. It is hard to forget this wonderful smell! How can this image of being the fragrance of Christ, by our lives marked with joy, simplicity, peace, and hope (to name a few) make the gospel advance in the world around you?

Pray About

> How have you experienced the fragrance of Christ in others?
>
> How can you accompany someone on their faith journey, sharing the gospel without words?

Entrusting Ourselves to Mary

I believe that an effective way to keep our lives saturated with the fragrance of the gospel is to entrust ourselves to the Virgin Mary—to let ourselves be educated by her. We are living in the times of Mary. We have to be guided by her. Mary is entirely filled with the perfume of the gospel—with gentleness, love, goodness, peace, and humility. She knows how to share with us the good fragrance of Christ with which she's filled, and she can help us preserve it and not be contaminated by the spirit of the world.

Jesus says to us, "I send you out like lambs in the midst of wolves" (Luke 10:3, NABRE). I was reflecting on this and asking myself, "What is most dangerous thing for a sheep that is among wolves?" I concluded that it's not to be eaten—because for us, this is a grace; it is martyrdom. But what is most dangerous for the sheep is to become a wolf—to be contaminated by violence, by fear, by everything around us. This is our big challenge today: to keep our hearts pure and free of pride, fear, discouragement, human ambition, and human security—to not compromise

The more we belong to the Blessed Virgin Mary, the more we will find in her all that we need for the proclamation of the gospel.

with the spirit of the world, but to be faithful to the spirit of the gospel. This can be difficult.

We cannot evangelize without Mary. It is through her that Jesus came into the world. It is also through her that Jesus will reveal himself to all good, willing hearts. And the more we belong to the Blessed Virgin Mary, the more we will experience her protection and maternal tenderness and find in her all that we need for the proclamation of the gospel: faithfulness to prayer, strength of faith, purity of love, gentleness, humility, peace, courage, and the ability to give our lives for the Lord and for our brothers and sisters.

St. Louis-Marie Grignion de Montfort was a beautiful apostle of the consecration to Mary. He was also an evangelist who went on many missions. He asked the pope to allow him to be a missionary abroad, but the pope said, "No, the need is great for you to be a missionary in France." In his book, *True Devotion to the Blessed Virgin*, he wrote about the apostles of the last times. He wrote that there would be a new generation of apostles who would be given to the Church by Mary—men and women who live not according to the wisdom of the world, but according to the spirit of poverty and humility of the Beatitudes, and who are filled with the wisdom and strength of the Holy Spirit.[3]

New apostles are given to the Church by Mary. These are people who are simple, poor, and humble, but educated by Mary, filled with the Holy Spirit through his presence and their deep relationship with Mary. Where Mary is, the Holy Spirit comes

---

[3] St. Louis-Marie Grignion de Montfort, *A Treatise on the True Devotion to the Blessed Virgin* (London: Burns and Lambert, 1863), 35-36.

quickly and pours himself out. Mary also protects us, keeps us from the spirit of the world, and keeps in us this fragrance of the gospel, this simplicity and purity of heart we need so much. She will protect us from evil and from the contamination of the spirit of the world.

So let us entrust ourselves to Mary, that she may fashion us into the image of her Son and make us the apostles that the world needs today. I insist on this: we have to belong to Mary, to be consecrated to Mary, and to welcome Mary into our lives as Jesus invited the disciple John to do at the foot of the cross. This is such a great gift that Jesus gave us during the time of the redemption of the world, when he was about to die. Just before he said, "It is finished" (John 19:30), he said to Mary, "Behold, your son" (19:26). And he said to John, "Behold, your mother" (19:27). And John welcomed Mary as his mother.

We are invited in a very special way to welcome Mary as our mother. She will be a source of incredible power for us in the work of evangelization that is before us today, for the glory of God and the salvation of our brothers and sisters. Like St. John of the Cross said, "We don't want to go to heaven alone." We want everyone to be saved, to know the love and mercy of God. We want everyone to be purified, to be forgiven, and to be transformed by the power of the love of God.

We want a new Pentecost for the whole world, as the prophet says: "The glory of the Lord shall be revealed, / and all flesh shall see it together" (Isaiah 40:5). God is preparing a new Pentecost. There will be a time of suffering, of many martyrs. But there will also be an incredible outpouring of the Holy Spirit, a Pentecost of mercy. Mary is the one chosen to prepare this Pentecost of mercy. She is inviting so many poor, simple, and wounded people to join her army.

And we can be sure that, with Mary, God will have the victory over the power of Satan. We are full of joy and hope because of the great things God is doing today. We want to be part of it, according to our abilities, our work, and our commitments, but also with the assurance that we are who we are supposed to be: Christians anointed with the grace of the Holy Spirit.

Reflect

> How have you experienced the characteristics of Mary—fathfulness to prayer, strength of faith, and purity of love, to name a few—at work in your life?
>
> How can Mary help you keep your heart free from fear, discouragement, human ambition, and the spirit of the world?

Pray About

> Invite Mary to guide you into her way of sharing the gospel.
>
> Take some time to contemplate "the great things God is doing today," and the promise that, with Mary, God will have the victory over the enemy's power.

Q & A with Fr. Jacques Philippe

How can we be more pure in heart?

Purity of heart is a gift from God, so we have to ask for it! In the psalms, David said, "Create in me a clean heart" (51:10). So a pure heart is also a creation of God. I think perhaps the most important aspect of purity is not to be perfect, because the truth is that we are poor—we are sinners. But rather, to have a heart that not divided between God and the world. A man that is pure in heart is not a perfect man, but he is a person who has made the choice for God—he is completely decided for God.

In addition, the person who is pure in heart is faithful to prayer, because this purity of heart is not something I can build by myself, but I have to receive it. If I am in communication with God, the purity of God is pouring into my heart, little by little. It takes time. It's like an infusion when I am sick. It comes drop by drop. The purity of God is entering into me—through prayer, the sacraments, the Eucharist, and Confession. Every time I confess my sins, every time I receive the Eucharist, the purity of God is being infused into me.

And also, it is important to accept our need for growth and change. When I am living with the Lord, when I am going about my days and meeting new people, if I have a desire for the truth and if I am sincere, I will become more and more aware of my hardness of heart, my pride, and my difficulty in loving people. I will begin to see my sin more clearly—what is wounded in me. I will realize how proud I am or how impatient I am, and the wrongs that I have to forgive.

But all the impurity I see in myself should not discourage me. As soon as I realize my sin and my lack of holiness, my task is to offer it to God, to pray, "God, I am so hard of heart; I'm so proud. I have difficulty forgiving. I offer this to you because you are the source of purity; you are the source of salvation." As we do this, little by little the grace of the Holy Spirit will purify and transform our lives. And we have to be patient with ourselves, confident in God, and simply use the means that God is giving us to acquire this inner purity.

Every morning, I have the choice to choose God. Every single morning, I can choose God. I can choose faith. I can choose love. My choice is good for twenty-four hours. And then the next day, I can do it again. This is how, day after day, with great patience and commitment, I can persevere and never become discouraged. We must know that our biggest enemy in the spiritual life is discouragement. So we don't get discouraged; we don't fear. We trust God. And day by day, we choose the gospel.

What is the connection between public prayer and evangelization?

I think public prayer is very important because the testimony of people praying together can be very touching. For example, many people in the Slavic countries were evangelized when they saw the beautiful liturgy in the Hagia Sophia in Constantinople. A beautiful liturgy can be very touching for people. In the story of the Church, sometimes people have been converted by the beauty of singing or the fervor of people or seeing a big assembly of people praising God with joy. Also, when people pray together, there is a strength in the prayer. Jesus said, "For where two or three are gathered in my name, there am I in the midst of them" (Matthew 18:20). And "if two of you agree on earth about anything they ask, it will be done for them by my Father in heaven" (18:19).

Every time we pray together in community, we strengthen our faith, our hope, and our love. When I am praying alone, I can easily become discouraged and sad. But when I have brothers and sisters to pray with, our faith strengthens one another, and there is a reciprocal encouragement and sustaining. We cannot be alone in our Christian faith. We have to gather with brothers and sisters to pray and to support one another. Public prayer has a great importance in evangelization because it is strengthening the people's faith and is a beautiful testimony of God in unity and prayer.

What is the role of private prayer in the work of evangelization?

Both public and private times of prayer are very important. I cannot only be satisfied with public prayer. If there is no private prayer, even my public prayer will not be deep. Private prayer gives depth, intensity, and faithfulness to public prayer. I have to have brothers and sisters to pray with, I have to belong to the Church, but I also have to have my personal prayer. Not everyone prays in private in the same way, but it's very important to be in contact with the Lord in a time of silence and intimacy with God for at least fifteen minutes a day.

When I was twenty-three years old, I experienced a difficult time in my life. I went on a retreat at a monastery, and there I felt, in a very clear way but not audibly, that Jesus was telling me to take fifteen minutes every day with him. He didn't ask for more or less, just fifteen minutes a day. And those fifteen minutes changed my life. Little by little, I was able to give space to the Lord in my life. I received more hope and courage.

So personal prayer is very important. There, the Holy Spirit speaks to us and changes our hearts. And the closer we are to God, the closer we are to people. The more attentive we are to God in our personal prayer life, the more we will be able to be attentive to people's needs. We receive light, strength, and God's presence in prayer. It is the source of every good thing.

How do I resist the temptation to be overly focused on my own plans and activities in evangelization?

The plans and activities that we make are important. We have to be generous and creative with our time. We cannot stay in our rooms; we have to go out and try to reach people. To do this, we have to prepare ourselves and also to explore what is possible within our country or parish. Love is active.

But it is important to understand that what we are doing cannot be fruitful if our foundation is not love of God and the presence of the Holy Spirit in our hearts. I have been insisting a lot on these things: prayer, intimacy with God, inner transformation, and seeking purity of heart, because sometimes, when somebody is doing and doing, they don't realize the deeper intention of their heart. Sometimes they don't realize their deeper motives. Sometimes their generosity isn't pure. Sometimes they want accolades, to be recognized. There may be self-seeking in what they are doing.

Our intentions can be mixed. So prayer helps us be purified little by little from this, to be more clear and more pure in what we do, and also to receive discernment from the Holy Spirit. Very often when we have something to do, we want to be creative, but we also have to receive inspiration from the Holy Spirit in what we say and what we do—in our decisions and our plans. It's very important to receive inspiration from God. This isn't to say I don't have to use my brain, but it's very important that we be guided and strengthened by the presence of the Holy Spirit. The Holy Spirit is primarily received in prayer.

How do we help people who are distracted by technology to experience God's presence?

This is a very big challenge today. We have to invite people to have discipline with the use of their devices. One way we can do this is by helping them taste how beautiful it can be to be in silence, in prayer, and to be open to God's presence. It is important for them is to be able to take a time of silence and prayer during a retreat or outside in nature. We can help them by not only telling them about the dangers of technology, but also by helping them to taste God's presence.

Silence can be filled with something beautiful. Prayer can be a joy. So we can help people to gather together, with someone to guide them, to experience that it is beautiful to be together with the Lord and to have times of prayer and adoration and praise. We can give them a taste of God's presence. This can help them detach from too much social media and to take time to stay in the presence of God. What can also help them is contact with nature. Since we are always looking at screens, walking in the forest or contemplating the sea can be the first steps to contemplating the presence of God. Nature can be a very beautiful experience of God's presence and power.

Nine Days to Rediscover the Joy of Prayer
ISBN: 9781594173356

Nine Days to Welcome Peace
ISBN: 9781594173653

Nine Days to Strengthen Your Faith
ISBN: 9781594173974

Priestly Fatherhood: Treasure in Earthen Vessels
ISBN: 9781594174179

Interior Freedom
ISBN: 9781594170522

The Way of Trust and Love
ISBN: 9781594171659

Real Mercy
ISBN: 9781594172472

Books by Fr. Jacques Philippe

Trusting God in the Present

Life is always full of new and unexpected challenges, but each challenge is also an opportunity to draw closer to God. Fr. Jacques Philippe shows you how to maintain peace of heart through turbulent times and discern the choices that will be helpful for you and others. God is with you, and he is inviting you to a new perspective, renewed hope, and a more abundant life.
 # BJPSE2   ISBN: 9781593257040

**To order, visit www.wau.org/books or call 301-874-1700.
Bulk discounts are available when ordering by phone.**

Also by Fr. Jacques Philippe

To order these books, visit scepterpublishers.org or call 800-322-8773.

Searching for and Maintaining Peace
ISBN: 9780818909061

In the School of the Holy Spirit
ISBN: 9781594170539

Time for God
ISBN: 9781594170669

Called to Life
ISBN: 9781594170690

Thirsting for Prayer
ISBN: 9781594172083

Fire & Light: Learning to Receive the Gift of God
ISBN: 9781594172533

The Eight Doors of the Kingdom: Meditations on the Beatitudes
ISBN: 9781594172755

The Word Among Us publishes a monthly devotional magazine, books, Bible studies, and pamphlets that help Catholics grow in their faith.

To learn more about who we are and what we publish, visit www.wau.org. There you will find a variety of Catholic resources that will help you grow in your faith.

Your review makes a difference! If you enjoyed this book, please consider sharing your review on Amazon using the QR code below.

Embrace His Word
Listen to God . . .

www.wau.org

www.ingramcontent.com/pod-product-compliance
Lightning Source LLC
Chambersburg PA
CBHW050046080526
44586CB00014B/1477